It is important to know the following in order to understand what you read:

Who is the story about?
What happened in the story?
Where did it happen?
When did it happen?

A Baby Panda

One special day in April, far away in China, a baby panda was born. The tiny panda weighed only about four ounces (113 grams), and her eyes were closed. Even though the baby panda grew quickly, she was helpless for a long time.

When she was three months old, she had hair and could crawl. By the time the baby was seven months old, she was able to run, climb, and begin eating bamboo. In about a year she would be ready to leave her mother.

1. **Who** is the story about?

_____

2. **Where** did the story take place?

_____

3. **When** did the story happen?

_____

4. **What** was happening to the baby panda?

_____

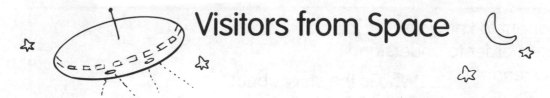

Visitors from Space

It was 2:00 in the morning when Robot M6-D6 landed his spacecraft outside Greg's window. The pale-green light from the spacecraft's anti-gravity blasters caused Greg to wake up. He peered carefully through the window and tried to decide if he should go outside. As he watched, a silver ramp dropped from the bottom of the spacecraft and out rolled M6-D6.

Soon Greg's curiosity was too much for him. He crept out to get a closer look at the visitor. Greg hid behind the woodpile and watched as M6-D6 rolled around the yard picking up samples of rocks and small plants.

As Greg leaned over the woodpile to get a closer look, he knocked over several pieces of wood. The noise startled M6-D6 and he began to beep loudly. The robot hurried to the spacecraft. A moment later, the yard was lit by a pale-green glow. Soon the spacecraft was gone.

1. **Who** are the characters in this story?

_____

2. **When** did the story take place?

_____

3. **What** caused Greg to wake up?

_____

4. **Where** did the spacecraft land?

_____

5. **What** was the purpose of M6-D6's trip to Earth?

_____

6. **What** caused M6-D6 to leave so suddenly?

_____

It is important to know **why** something happens in order
to understand what you read.

The Lion and the Mouse

One hot summer afternoon, a fierce lion was napping in the shade.
A small mouse, out looking for a bit of lunch, ran right across the lion.
The mouse didn't see the danger until it was too late. He was caught in
the lion's paw. "Please don't eat me," begged the little mouse. "Let me
go and someday I will repay you." The lion roared with laughter. "How
can a little thing like you ever help the King of Beasts?" Still laughing,
the lion let the frightened mouse go.

Several weeks later, the lion found himself trapped in a hunter's net.
He roared and roared as he tried to break the strong ropes. The lion's
terrible cries were heard by the little mouse. The mouse thought, "That
is the lion that let me go. I must see if I can help him." He rushed to
where the lion was caught and began to gnaw at the ropes. Before
long the lion was free. "See. I told you I would repay you some day,"
said the mouse. "Even a tiny mouse can sometimes help the King of
Beasts."

1. **Why** did the mouse get caught by the lion?

_____

2. **Why** did the lion roar with laughter?

_____

3. **Why** did the King of Beasts need the mouse's help?

_____

Koalas

You can use the material you are reading to help figure out the meaning of words you might not know.

Read this story about a koala. Think about what you read. This will help you to figure out the meaning of the underlined words. Write what the words mean on page 5.

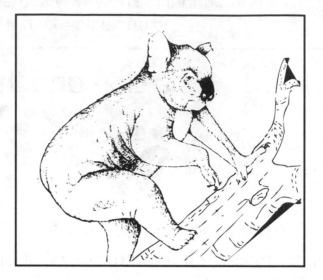

Although koalas resemble bears, they are <u>marsupials</u>. Marsupial comes from a word meaning "pouch." Koalas, therefore, are related to kangaroos, opossums, and <u>wombats</u>, but not to bears. The name koala comes from a word used by the native people of Australia. In the <u>Aboriginal</u> langauge, the word means "no water" or "no drink." Koalas are found in the coastal areas of northeast and southern Australia. Koalas live in <u>eucalyptus</u> forests.

Because they spend most of their lives in trees, koalas are called "<u>arboreal</u>" animals. Koalas eat eucalyptus leaves, shoots, bark, and flowers. The water in the leaves is all the koala needs. The oil in the leaves gives the koalas a strong odor, something like a type of cough drop. Koalas are <u>nocturnal</u> feeders, eating at night and sleeping during the day.

Koalas are well suited to life in the trees. They are remarkable climber. The toes of the koala are perfect for a tree dwelling animal. The toes are made of two sections which can be moved together in a "pinching" motion. These <u>opposing</u> toes with their razor sharp claws enable the koala to securely grip branches. When climbing, the koala holds and pulls with its forelegs and pushes with its rear legs. The rear legs can also hold onto the trunk, freeing the forelegs for other activities.

Use clues from the story on page 4 to help you understand what these words mean. Write what you can tell about each word.

1. marsupial _____

2. wombat _____

3. aboriginal _____

4. eucalyptus _____

5. arboreal _____

6. nocturnal _____

7. opposing _____

Now, pick three of the words and write your own sentences to show you understand their meaning.

1. _____

_____

2. _____

_____

3. _____

_____

Main Ideas and Supporting Details

Main ideas are the BIG and IMPORTANT ideas.
Details are extra information added to make the main idea clearer.
Most stories have a few main ideas and many supporting details.

Read the story below.
Underline what you think is the **main idea** in each paragraph.

The Rhinoceros

The two species of rhinoceros living in Africa are different in several ways. One type is the black or long-lipped rhino. It is a browsing animal and uses its long, upper lip to grab leaves from bushes and pull them into its mouth. The other type is the white or square-mouthed rhino. It is a grazer and uses its wide mouth to bite off many blades of grass at one time.

A rhino is a strange-looking animal. The wrinkled nose with its two vertical horns takes up most of its face. The short, clumsy-looking legs seem too small to hold up the rhino's immense, solid body. Its thick, rough skin hangs in loose folds with no hair to soften the surface.

Even though a rhino looks clumsy and slow, it can run as fast as a horse for a short distance. The black rhino often has to use its short legs to escape from hunters. A rhino has good hearing, but poor vision. If it is startled, it is apt to make a sudden charge at the intruder.

A rhino rests most of the day and is active at night, when it eats grass, leafy twigs, and shrubs. It uses its long digging horn to uproot plants and overturn bushes and trees. The rhino likes to find a water hole where it can drink and take the mudbaths that help keep its skin cool.

- The next page gives the main ideas of this story.
- Read the **main idea** for each paragraph and write one or more **supporting details** for each one.
- Read the story again if you need help remembering the details.

Paragraph 1

Main Idea: The two kinds of African rhinos are different in several ways.

Supporting Details: _____

_____

_____

Paragraph 2

Main Idea: Rhinos are unusual looking animals.

Supporting Details: _____

_____

_____

Paragraph 3

Main Idea: Rhinos are not slow and clumsy.

Supporting Details: _____

_____

_____

Paragraph 4

Main Idea: Rhinos are most active at night.

Supporting Details: _____

_____

_____

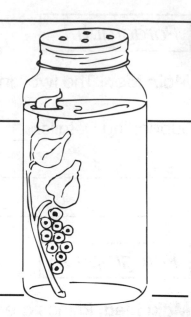

Story Sequence

The **sequence** of a story is the order in which the events occur.

The Science Project

Read this story, and then number the sentences on the next page in the correct order.

Just before the bell rang, Mr. Nielsen said, "Don't forget that your science projects are due a week from today."

Jose thought about his project. A few days ago he had found some frog eggs at the pond near his house. He had scooped up a dozen or so with some pond water in an empty jar. At home, he placed the jar on top of the refrigerator to stay warm. The eggs looked like small black beads in white jelly.

Each day Jose looked at the eggs through a magnifying glass and drew what he saw. Day by day, he watched the jelly part of the egg get smaller as the tadpole grew in the black center. A head and tail could be seen and soon the tadpoles began to move. His science book said that the jelly part was food for the growing tadpole.

The next Thursday the first of the eggs hatched. A tiny tadpole stuck itself to a leaf of the pond plant Jose had put in the jar. It had no mouth yet, but Jose could see finger-like gills behind its head.

By Friday, four more eggs had hatched. Jose carefully carried the jar to school, along with his day-by-day drawings and written record of the changes he'd seen.

"This is a fine project, Jose," said Mr. Nielsen. "You must have given it a lot of thought."

Number these sentences about *The Science Project* in the order they happened in the story.

____3____ After several days the tadpoles began to hatch.

____5____ On Friday, Jose took his science project to school.

____6____ Mr. Nielsen liked Jose's science project.

____1____ Jose found frog eggs in the pond and took some home in a jar.

____4____ The young tadpoles had gills, but no mouth.

____2____ Each day the black part ot the eggs grew to look more like a tadpole.

Make a drawing to illustrate Jose's science project.

Story Sequence

One way to figure out sequence is to look for hints such as these words:

after	**before**	**soon**	**at 3 o'clock**
first	**finally**	**in the morning**	**breakfast**
lunch	**dinner**	**then**	**at noon**

Read these sentences. Number the sentences in the correct sequence to tell a story.

6   After lunch, Jeanne went to play at the park with Lee.

3   She ate a big bowl of oatmeal with raisins for breakfast.

1   On Saturday, Jeanne had a great day.

9   Soon it was time for bed and sweet dreams.

4   Then she helped her mother make cookies for lunch.

2   When she got up in the morning, she put on her best shirt and shorts.

7   At 4 o'clock it was time to go home and get ready for dinner.

5   For lunch, Jeanne ate a banana, a sandwich, and three cookies.

8   Jeanne played video games with her brother after dinner.

Cause and Effect

A **cause** is what makes something happen.
Not looking where I was going **caused** *me to run into the door.*
An **effect** is what happened.
The **effect** of not looking was that I ran into the door.

It is important to understand what **effects** are caused by events in the story. To find the **cause**, ask yourself,

"Why did this happen?"

Read these sentences.
Look for the cause and the effect.

1. After the rain, there were many accidents on the
   slick streets of the city.

   cause - _____

   effect - _____

2. Polly knew the water was boiling when she heard
   the teakettle whistle.

   cause - _____

   effect - _____

3. Toby had to be taken to the hospital after he fell out
   of the tall tree in his backyard.

   cause - _____

   effect - _____

Sometimes a **cause** will result in more than one **effect**.
After the rain, the sidewalks were wet, and the streets were slick.

Cause: rain   **Effect:** wet sidewalks
                                           slick streets

Read the selection below, then write
the **cause** beside each **effect** listed.

Hurricane!

A hurricane has an awesome destructive power. The towering cloud masses produce heavy rains. The rain, combined with the strong winds, can damage plants and buildings. Automobile accidents occur on the slippery streets. The powerful winds build up huge waves on the ocean surface. These waves endanger ships in the area. They also result in extremely high storm tides rising along the shore. The high water can destroy property and take lives.

Cause:	Effect:
1. _____	heavy rains
2. _____	damage to plants and buildings
3. _____	automobile and human accidents
4. _____	huge waves
5. _____	endangered ships
6. _____	storm tide
7. _____	property destruction and deaths

Hercules

When the soil begins to warm each spring, my sister Denise and I start planning our garden. We spend hours drawing our plan on graph paper until we've decided exactly which flowers and vegetables we want to plant. Then we search through a pile of seed catalogs and order the seeds we will need.

As last summer's hard work was about to pay off, a disaster befell our garden.

Denise had gone to the garden to pick lettuce for a salad. I heard her shriek and charged out of the house, unable to imagine what was wrong. There stood Denise, mouth agape, in front of a bare area of dirt that had been our lettuce patch. There was no lettuce!

After staring in bewilderment for some time, we sized up the situation. There are no rabbits where we live; there was no evidence of gopher activity. Yet there was no lettuce.

The next morning our cabbage had disappeared; the following day, tomatoes on low-hanging branches were gone. By the third day, we were no longer in a state of shock. We were mad as hornets. Denise said we should stake out the garden at night and trap the culprit.

That night we crouched in the bushes near the garden, flashlights on ready, waiting for the who-or-whatever was destroying our hard work. Just as we were about to throw in the towel, a faint crunching sound came from the broccoli row. Two beams of light flashed, revealing a large turtle with a broccoli stalk dangling from his mouth. While I held my light on the turtle, Denise ran to get Dad and the old hamster cage.

The whole family gathered in the garage to take stock of this garden wrecker that Dad had carefully caged. The reptile was big. The span of his shell was close to a foot. When his head poked out of his shell, his little, beady eyes blinked at us. I think he was as surprised by the situation as we were.

"If I'm not mistaken," said Dad, "this is a desert tortoise, not a turtle. How he got here is certainly a mystery."

The next day Denise and I rode our bikes to the animal shelter to ask what to do with our visitor. Denise had seen tortoises at the shelter when her class had been there on a field trip. The woman in the education department politely listened to our story.

"Yes," she replied. "Your visitor surely sounds like a desert tortoise. Most of the tortoises that end up in our part of the country have been brought home by people who visit the desert. They don't realize that it isn't healthy for the tortoises to be removed from their environment. When they find out how hard it is to care for a large tortoise, they just let them go, thinking they'll do fine on their own. They don't think about what it's like where the tortoise lives—sandy and warm all year."

"The worst part is that tortoises can't be returned to the desert once they've been away from it. In our climate, tortoises get a virus which doesn't harm them usually, but would kill other tortoises in the desert."

She also told us that tortoises can live to be over one hundred years old. We looked at the three tortoises that lived in the shelter. We were told that the shelter would be happy to give "our" tortoise a home. That very afternoon we delivered our midnight muncher to the shelter. The shelter named him Hercules. I don't suppose anyone can tell when a tortoise is happy, but I know we were.

Number the sentences in the order they happened in the story:

_____ We caught and caged a large tortoise.

_____ We looked forward to our garden's harvest each year.

_____ We planned to catch the destroyer of our garden.

_____ The lettuce was the first to disappear.

_____ We learned that the tortoise could not be returned to the desert.

_____ The shelter agreed to provide our tortoise with a home.

_____ We went to the animal shelter to find out what to do with the tortoise.

Think about this: You learned many facts about desert tortoises from this story. Write four of the facts you learned.

1. _____

_____

2. _____

_____

3. _____

_____

4. _____

_____

Answer these questions about *Hercules*.

1. After all their hard work planting and caring for their garden, what disaster happened?

   _____

   _____

2. How did the children catch Hercules?

   _____

   _____

3. How did Hercules probably get from the desert to their garden?

   _____

   _____

4. Why couldn't Hercules ever be returned to the desert?

   _____

   _____

5. What solution was found to the problem of what to do with Hercules?

   _____

   _____

The story said the children were "as mad as hornets" because their garden was being destroyed. We have many colorful expressions that compare people's behavior to animals. These are called <u>similes</u>. Fill in each of these blanks with a kind of animal to create more similes.

as mad as a _____   as slow as a _____

as busy as a _____   as meek as a _____

as fat as a _____   as strong as an_____

as sly as a _____   as quiet as a _____

as stubborn as a _____   waddled like a _____

as cute as a _____ in a rug

Word Box

fox	bee	mouse	ox
hornet	bug	mule	snail
lamb	duck	pig	

Choose three similes.
Write a sentence with each one to show you understand what it means.

1. _____

_____

2. _____

_____

3. _____

_____

Aisle Search

Beth's family moved from their apartment to a new house. They needed to build a fence around their yard so they could adopt a dog. While Beth's parents bought the lumber and cement, Beth looked for the other supplies they needed. A sign in the store listed the kinds of merchandise found in each aisle. The aisles were numbered.

Aisle Numbers

Building Tools	Aisle 6
Lighting	Aisle 2
Hardware for Gates	Aisle 3
Paints and Stains	Aisle 12
Plants	Aisle 10
Electrical Supplies	Aisle 15
Nails, Screws, Bolts, Building Hardware	Aisle 4
Plumbing Supplies	Aisle 1
Protective Clothing	Aisle 11
Fireplace Supplies	Aisle 7
Step Stools and Ladders	Aisle 5
Garden Supplies	Aisle 9

Write the aisle number for each item on Beth's list.

two hammers _____

drill and drill bits _____

ladder _____

waterproof stain for the wood _____

pliers _____

nails, screws, bolts _____

a hand saw _____

a tool box _____

3 pair of gloves _____

hinges and a lock for the gate _____

Drawing a Map

Maggie plans to walk to Julia's house Saturday afternoon to work on a science project. On Friday, Julia gave her written directions from the school to her house. Maggie decided to draw a map from the directions. She thought it would be easier to follow the map when she walked to Julia's house.

Read the directions Julia gave to Maggie. Draw a map showing the route from Washington School to Julia's house. Label the streets. Use symbols for the stores, the post office, and the stop sign. You may invent your own symbols. Add a legend to the bottom of your map to explain what the symbols mean. For example, you might write an S where the stop sign is or draw a stamped envelope to represent the post office.

The Directions to Julia's House

- Walk to the corner of Elm and Walnut to Washington School.
- Cross the street and walk three blocks North on Walnut Street.
- Turn to the right on Cedar Street.
- Walk two blocks past Food Land, Video Center, the post office, and the park.
- Turn right at the stop sign on to Peach Tree Lane.
- Walk one block to Plum Court, which is on the right side of the street.
- My house number is 691. It's the second house on the left side of the court.

Legend

Ⓧ Washington School

Food Land

Video Center

Post Office

park

stop sign

Julia's House

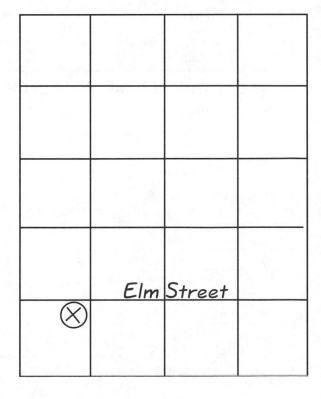

Elm Street

Find the Synonym

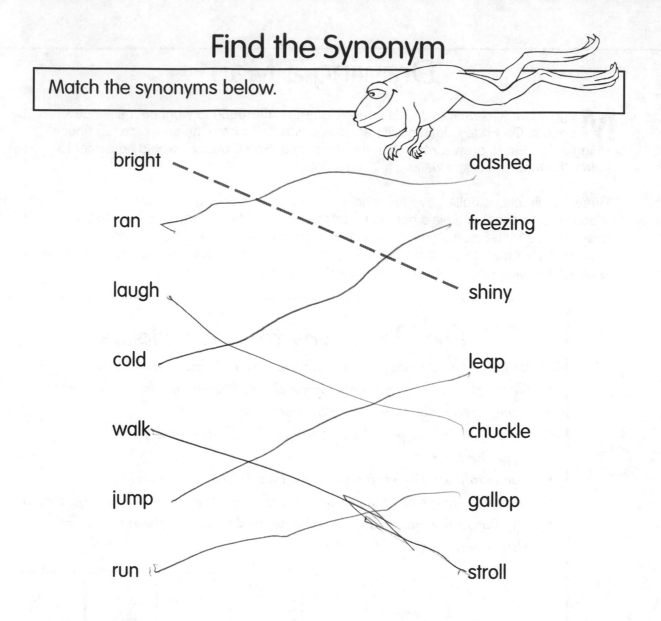

bright	dashed
ran	freezing
laugh	shiny
cold	leap
walk	chuckle
jump	gallop
run	stroll

Write a sentence with each of these words to show you know
its meaning.

chuckle 1. _____

dashed 2. _____

gallop 3. _____

Use synonyms for the underlined words in the clues to help you complete this puzzle.

Across

2. Jan wore a <u>colorful</u> outfit to the party.
3. The children <u>ran</u> around the park.
5. His story was so <u>absurd</u> we didn't believe it was true.
6. I had to <u>laugh</u> when I saw the clown.
7. The horse began to <u>run</u> around the corral.
9. He plans to <u>give</u> money to that charity.
10. It's fun to <u>stroll</u> along the path at dawn.
11. The <u>huge</u> gorilla was sleeping in a tall tree.

Down

1. The <u>cold</u> weather told us winter was here.
4. Max felt <u>terrible</u> after he yelled at his friend.
6. Please help me <u>select</u> a gift for my dad.
8. Carlos' dog can <u>jump</u> over the backyard fence.

Word Box

awful
bright
choose
chuckle
dashed
donate
enormous
freezing
gallop
leap
silly
walk

Find the Antonyms

colorful   late

huge   guilty

early   dull

least   bored

innocent   tiny

contented   greatest

Write a sentence with each of these words to show you know its meaning.

chuckle   1. _____

_____

dashed   2. _____

_____

gallop   3. _____

_____

Use antonyms for the underlined words to help you complete this puzzle.

Across

1. The stream was <u>gushing</u> over the rocks.
5. Jane was <u>late</u> for school.
6. <u>Tiny</u> stars decorated the poster.
7. She was very <u>healthy</u> all year.
9. His tie had a <u>colorful</u> pattern.
10. Candles made the room look <u>cheerful</u>.
11. Do you think he is <u>guilty</u>?

Down

2. She is <u>polite</u> to everyone.
3. The movie was <u>boring</u>.
4. The cold rain made the day seem <u>gloomy</u>.
8. He had to <u>open</u> the door for the old man.

Word Box

cheerful
close
dull
early
gloomy
huge
innocent
interesting
rude
sick
trickling

Homophone Fun

Use these homophones to fill the blanks on the next page.

berry = small fruit
bury = cover completely

flea = insect
flee = run away

hall = long, narrow room
haul = move to another place

heal = get well
heel = back of the foot

loan = give temporarily
lone = by oneself

main = most important
mane = lots of hair

pole = pillar
poll = survey

role = part you play
roll = list/bun

pore = tiny opening in the skin
pour = dispense

sole = bottom of the foot/the only one
soul = spirit

Remember.....homophones are words that sound
alike but have different meanings and spellings.

Fill in the blanks. Use the homophones on the previous page to help you fill in the blanks.

1. Did the cut on your _____heel_____ _____heal_____ yet?

2. I cannot _____loan_____ you the _____lone_____ dollar in my pocket!

3. If you _____bury_____ the ripe _____berry_____, no one can eat it.

4. The male lion's _____mane_____ is his _____main_____ feature.

5. Please _____haul_____ those things from the _____hall_____ to the garage.

6. A special collar will cause the _____fleas_____s to _____flee_____ from your dog.

7. Please _____pour_____ some lotion on my hand to soften the _____pore_____s of my skin.

8. Take a _____poll_____ of the class opinions and post it on that _____pole_____.

Compound Words

Compound words are made of two smaller words put together.

wheel + chair = **wheelchair**
grand + mother = **grandmother**
holy + day =   **holiday**

Put two words together to make new words.

basket + ball = _ _ basketball_ _

cheer + leader = _____

wild + life = _____

house + work = _____

high + way = _____

news + cast = _____

week + end = _____

wood + land = _____

home + made = _____

who + ever = _____

touch + down = _____

under + ground = _____

ware + house = _____

well - l + fare = _____

Contractions

Contractions are words made by putting two words together, but adding an apostrophe in the place of some of the letters.

Match the two words to the correct contractions.

was + not	we're
could + not	he's
were + not	wasn't
we + are	couldn't
he + is	weren't
of + the + clock	can't
they + will	you've
you + have	it's
it + is	o'clock
can + not	they'll
will + not	I'd
is + not	isn't
I + would	won't

Prefixes

A **prefix** is added to the beginning of a word.
A **prefix** can change the meaning of a word.

interesting becomes ***un**interesting*

The prefixes **un**, **in** and **im** mean **not** and, when added to words, change them into their antonym.

Add **prefixes** to the words below to make **antonyms**,
then write the meanings of each new word.

1. **in** + effective = _____

meaning:

2. **im** + personal = _____

meaning:

3. **un** + likely = _____

meaning:

4. **un** + comfortable = _____

meaning:

5. **in** + secure = _____

meaning:

6. **im** + perfect = _____

meaning:

Suffix

A suffix is a syllable put at the end of a word to change its meaning or give more information. Here are some common suffixes we use.

ful	less	es	ess	ly	able
est	ology	let	ment	ness	ant

Underline the suffix in these words.

care<u>less</u>   owlet   heaviest   slowly

speechless   watchful   happiness   careful

profitable   bosses   servant   sadness

happily   biology   quickest   governess

Write the words next to the clues.

__watchful__ keeping an eye on things

_____ unable to talk

_____ successful business

_____ a small owl

_____ a state of pleasure

_____ most rapid

_____ sorrow

_____ weighs the most

_____ not very quick

Help!

You are trapped in a supermarket.
Write about your adventure.

Be sure that your story tells:
- how you happened to get locked in
- what you will do
- your plan for escape
- how you actually got out

Planet Earth

You have just landed on Earth from a distant planet.
What do you think are the best things about the planet Earth?
What things are the worst?
Write a report back to the science exploration team on your planet.

Log of: _____

Science Officer: _____

Date: _____

Observations: _____

_____

_____

_____

_____

_____

_____

_____

Advice for Lonely

You are the columnist who gives advice to people who write to your newspaper. You have just received this letter from Lonely. Please answer it.

Dear Advice Columnist,

I have a problem. I'm having a hard time meeting and keeping friends. What should I do? Help! I need your advice.

Signed,

Dear Lonely,

Frankenstein Night

Mary Shelley, born on August 30, 1797, wrote the novel Frankenstein over 160 years ago. It is a famous story about a monster that was made from parts of dead bodies by a scientist. The monster's name is really Adam, but most people call him Frankenstein. Just reading about what the monster is like sends shivers up and down your spine.

Think about a time when you were frightened and write to tell all about it.

Shivers

_____

_____

_____

_____

_____

_____

_____

What Animal Are You Like?

Compare yourself to an animal.
Tell how you are like that animal
and in what ways you are different.

Recipe for a Sandwich

November 3 is the day we salute John Montague, the Fourth Earl of Sandwich. He invented the sandwich. In his honor, develop a new sandwich. Draw a diagram that shows its layers. Then write a recipe for all those who would like to try it out.

My Sandwich

diagram:

I named it:

_____

You will need:

_____

_____

_____

_____

_____

_____

Here's how to make it:

_____

_____

_____

_____

_____

Complete Sentences

A **complete sentence** tells:
- who or what the sentence is about
- the action that is taking place

I am sitting on a tack.

Look at the groups of words below.
Put a circle around the complete sentences.
Cross out the groups of words that are only parts of sentences.

1. on the soccer field

2. marcus went into the store

3. my best friend

4. do you want a slice of pepperoni pizza

5. let's paint our bikes a new color

6. in my backpack

7. the rock group was playing loud music

8. i flew in a jet plane to my grandfather's for summer vacation

Sentences

There are four kinds of sentences:

Statements tell or state something:
Toni went to the park after school.

Questions ask something:
Did Toni go to the park after school yesterday?

Command sentences command or make a request:
Don't go to the park today. Be careful.

Exclamations show strong emotion:
Going to the park after school is a great idea!

. — statement and command

? — question

! — exclamation

1. Is the cheetah the fastest land animal _____

3. Begin your science projects this week _____

4. Don't go so close to that steep cliff _____

5. Have you studied about dinosaurs in school _____

6. Where do gray whales go in the winter _____

Run-on Sentences

A **run-on sentence** is two sentences together without end punctuation to separate them.

run-on :

They were well-prepared they won the battle.

correct:

They were well-prepared. They won the battle.

Read the sentences out loud to hear where one sentence ends and a new one begins. Put in **capital letters** and **punctuation marks.**

1. We like hot weather. We always go to the beach.

2. The bean seed sprouted. It grew three inches.

3. The Nile River is very long. It is located in Africa.

4. it is fun to do a science project just find an interesting topic

5. she read an amazing story it told about the old west

The Strange Planet

Read the story out loud to hear where one sentence ends and a new one begins. Place **punctuation marks** and **capital letters** in this story.

what a strange place this is it doesn't look anything like Earth why is the sky so dark and the ground so bumpy

what's that i saw a furry shape dart behind the rocks over there it's moving closer help i can't get away my feet are caught in some weird sticky ooze can anyone hear me

wow what a scary dream that was i'm glad to be awake that's the last time I have a peanut butter and pickle sandwich before I go to bed

Subject and Predicate

Every sentence has two main parts:

The **subject** tells who or what the sentence is about.

The **predicate** tells what the subject does.

subject

<u>Snow White and the seven dwarves</u> ate dinner together.

predicate

The seven dwarves **ate all of the delicious dinner**.

Draw one line under the **subject**.
Draw two lines under the **predicate**.

1. The tiny insects scurried quickly from place to place.

2. Matt liked the peace and calm of the forest.

3. The pioneers in their covered wagons faced many dangers.

4. The natives of the tiny village celebrated with a great feast.

5. The dense, tropical rain forests of Brazil are disappearing.

6. The children in the class screamed for the winning team.

Write a sentence of your own. Underline its subject once and its predicate twice.

_____

_____

Singular and Plural Subjects

Most verbs use different forms with singular and plural subjects.

Singular subject - The <u>girl</u> **sings** beautifully.

Plural subject - The <u>girls</u> **sing** beautifully.

Circle the correct form of the verb to agree with the subject.

1. Mr. Tyson (*read, reads*) us a story every Friday after lunch.

2. They (*watch, watches*) the play quietly.

3. Pinwheels (*spin, spins*) around when the wind blows.

4. Pioneer stories (*is, are*) interesting and inspiring.

5. The students (*prepare, prepares*) for the assembly at 2:00.

Write sentences using these subjects.

wild animals	the explorer

1. _____

_____

2. _____

_____

Proper Nouns

All **nouns** name people, places, and things.
A **proper noun** names a particular person,
place, or thing and begins with a capital letter.

Margaret visited **N**ew **Y**ork **C**ity on the **F**ourth of **J**uly

Read these sentences.
Replace the underlined part with **proper nouns**.
Don't forget to begin each proper noun with a capital letter.

1. <u>The children</u> traded baseball cards and talked about the players.

   _____

2. The family went hiking in <u>a national park</u> on their vacation.

   _____

3. The teacher put <u>a game</u> on the table for free time.

   _____

4. The immigrants crossed the <u>ocean</u> and finally reached <u>a new land</u>.

_____   _____

Plural Nouns

Most **plural nouns** end in <u>s</u>, but some nouns form their plurals differently.

One	More than One
child	children
woman	women
man	men
foot	feet
ox	oxen
tooth	teeth
mouse	mice
goose	geese
moose	moose
fish	fish
deer	deer

foot

feet

Change each singular noun in the sentences below to its plural form.

1. All the (*man*) _____ and (*woman*)_____ at the meeting agreed with the motion.

2. The cats on the farm love to eat (*mouse*) _____ and (*fish*)_____.

3. Before the storm, the farmers herded all the (*goose*) _____ and (*ox*) _____ into the barn.

4. At bedtime, the children washed their (*foot*)_____ and brushed their (*tooth*) _____.

5. The children often saw groups of (*moose*) _____ and (*deer*) _____ in the forest.

Pronouns

Pronouns take the place of a noun. They are used:

1. in the place of the subject

    I you she he it we they

2. to show ownership

    my mine your yours his

    hers our ours their theirs

3. to receive the action of the verb or preposition

    me you her him us them

I like you.

Underline the **pronouns** in the sentences below.

Pronouns in the subject:

1. Joey and I went to the mall.

2. We bought ice-cream cones.

3. Joey and I asked for a new kitten.

Pronouns used to receive action:

1. Mom took Suzanne and me to the mall.

2. She bought us ice-cream cones.

3. Mom gave me a bandage for my hand.

Pronouns used to show ownership:

1. The students performed their play at 2 o'clock.

2. The dog wagged its tail when the girls came home.

3. We spent our summer vacation at Yosemite Park.

Adjectives

Adjectives are words that describe a noun or pronoun telling what kind, how many, or which one

green	**enormous**	**Italian**
eleven	**none**	**terrified**

Underline the **adjectives** in the sentences below. The number after the sentence tells how many adjectives you should find.

1. We wandered along the crowded wharf to watch the tall ships sail into the peaceful harbor. **(3)**

2. The weary pilgrims trudged through the driving rain. **(2)**

3. Holding the multi-colored flag high over the heads of the triumphant troops, the brave captain moved through the cheering crowd. **(4)**

4. The talented actress gladly accepted the challenging role in the new play. **(3)**

5. The victorious team raced off the muddy playing field. **(2)**

6. Throughout the long, stormy night, the excited campers shared ghost stories and old legends of mysterious events occuring in the ancient valley. **(7)**

Adverbs

An **adverb** describes the action of the verb, telling **how**, **when**, or **where** the action happened. Many times adverbs end with **y** or **ly**.

y or ly

Draw a circle around the adverbs in these sentences. Some sentences will have more than one.

1. The sun shone brightly on the blue water of the lake.

2. We walked quickly as the rain fell softly around us.

3. The teacher read us three funny stories today.

4. The Johnson family left for a camping trip yesterday.

Write sentences using three of these adverbs:

quietly	**too**	**often**
very	**honestly**	**never**

1. _____

_____

2. _____

_____

3. _____

_____

Commas

Use **commas** to separate:

- items in a series
  We ate **apples, dates, and nuts.**

- beginning words such as **yes, no,** and **well**
  Well, we might go to Yosemite.

- the person being addressed
  <u>**Susan**</u>, please bring me that tray.

Add **commas** where they are needed in the following sentences:

1. No they have not finished their homework yet.

2. We need to buy shirts pants socks and shoes for school.

3. Well you certainly did a good job on your science project.

4. Remember to bring your raincoat umbrella and hat.

5. Sam were you scared during that horror movie?

Write two sentences of your own that use **commas**.

1. _____

_____

2. _____

_____

"When Someone Speaks"

- Use quotation marks and a comma whenever you are repeating someone's exact words.

Mrs. Torres said, "Please close the door."

- Notice that a comma separates the words being spoken from the rest of the sentence.

Add quotation marks to these sentences.

1. "I'm tired of carrying this bag of grain," said the hen.

2. The dog said, "I won't carry it for you."

3. "Then I will eat all the bread myself," replied the hen.

4. The hen complained, "It is hard grinding the grain into bread."

5. The pig grunted, "Don't ask me to help!"

6. "Well, don't ask me for any of the bread when it's done," squawked the hen.

7. The other animals complained, "The hen is selfish to eat all the bread herself."

8. The hen thought, "If they had helped, I would be glad to share my bread."

Colons and Periods

A **colon** is used when writing the salutation of a business letter and to separate the hour from minutes when writing the time.

Dear Dr. Smith: **5:25 P.M.**

Add **colons** where they are needed in this letter.

Dear Professor Patterson:

Thank you for your help on my project. I will meet you at your office at 6:00.

Sincerely,
Jason Johnson

Use a **period** at the end of every abbreviation.

Prof. Salinas   **Mr. Edwards**

Add periods after the abbreviations in these sentences.

1. Rev Madison asked Ms Swanson to help him lead the singing.

2. Mr and Mrs Jamison left their keys in Ms Smith's car.

3. The students in Mr Jackson's class submitted their project to Prof Lowell to be judged.

4. The technician, Ms Rawlings, fixed our computer on Friday.

Alphabetical Order

You need to use **alphabetical order** to locate information in many kinds of reference sources.

Rewrite these animal names in alphabetical order.

zebra	1.	_____
badger	2.	_____
walrus	3.	_____
ferret	4.	_____
alligator	5.	_____
yak	6.	_____
pelican	7.	_____
gorilla	8.	_____
newt	9.	_____
dolphin	10.	_____
hippopotamus	11.	_____
salamander	12.	_____

Alphabetical Challenge

≠ When the first and second letters are the same -
  look at the **third** letter.
≠ When the first, second, and third letters are the same -
  look at the **fourth** letter.

Set 1:

crocus
crate
crustacean
crystal
creature
criminal

1. _____
2. _____
3. _____
4. _____
5. _____
6. _____

Set 2:

prepare
preacher
prevent
present
prey
precious

1. _____
2. _____
3. _____
4. _____
5. _____
6. _____

Using a Thesaurus

When you want to use a new word in place
of one you already know, look in a **thesaurus**.

A **thesaurus** lists synonyms (words with similar meanings).

Use the thesaurus on the next page to find a new word to replace the
underlined words in the sentences below.

1. Thomas felt great **fear** as he approached the cave.

   new word - _____

2. We saw a **white** figure moving across the lawn at midnight.

   new word - _____

3. The students **like** their new teacher.

   new word - _____

4. Cheetahs are very **fast** animals.

   new word - _____

5. **Throw** the ball to first base.

   new word - _____

6. Take off that **wet** jacket.

   new word - _____

7. We handled the kittens with **care.**

   new word - _____

Synonyms
are my
friends!

The Helpful Thesaurus

care   gentleness, attention, caution, thought

fast   rapid, swift, quick, fleet, speedy

fear   anxiety, terror, fright, alarm, dread

heavy   burdensome, weighty, hefty

like   admire, enjoy, be fond of

sign   token, symptom, symbol, badge, certificate

throw   hurl, toss, pass, heave, pitch, lob, chuck

wet   soaked, drenched, dripping, sodden, moist

white   pale, fair, ghostly, colorless

Parts of a Book

Most nonfiction books have several parts
which help you find information.

• Table of Contents
This is at the beginning of the book. It lists the titles of the chapters
and tells you the page on which each chapter begins.

• Index
This is at the end of the book. It lists the
topics in the book in alphabetical order
and gives you the pages on which you
will find each topic mentioned.

• Glossary
This is usually found at the back of the book.
It gives the meanings for important words
you need to understand as you read
the book.

What part of a book would you use to answer these questions?

1. Is an emu a bird or a mammal?

2. Is there a chapter on kangaroos?

3. Will this book tell me about Aborigines?

4. What do you do with a digeridoo?

5. Is the chapter on "The Outback" before
   or after the chapter on "The Great Barrier
   Reef"?

Using a Table of Contents

Table of Contents

1. What will you find out about in Chapter 3? _____

2. In which chapter will you find information
   about the Amazon River? _____

3. Name the chapter in which you will find
   information about how rivers are created. _____

4. In which chapter would you find out about
   waterfalls? _____

5. How many chapters are in this book ?
   _____

Using an Index

Rivers		Index	
Amazon River	76	estuaries	12
basin	18	irrigation	56
banks	5	levee	60
canyons	10	Nile River	72
cataracts	8	seaports	58
cities	57	silt	21
Colorado River	83	streams	17
course	4	transportation	60
dams	57	valley	35
deltas	16	waterfall	34
electricity	70	water power	70

1. On what page will you find information about ...?

   canyons _____10_____   cataracts _____8_____

   deltas _____16_____   dams _____57_____

   Nile River _____72_____

2. Where would you look to find out about how rivers are used to produce electricity?

   _____

3. Where would you look if you wanted to know about traveling on rivers?

   _____

4. Where would you look to find out the effect of silt on rivers?

   _____

Pictures, Captions, and Headings

Authors often give clues about their writing by providing **captions** for pictures and section **headings**. Studying these before you begin can help you understand what you are reading.

The polar bear blends well with the white snow around him.

What do you think the story will be about?

_____

Now read only the three **headings** on the next page.

• What does the first heading tell you about that section?

The section is about_____

• What do you think you will learn about in the second section?

I will read about _____

• What does the third heading tell you about the section?

This section tells about _____

The Polar Bear

A Cold World

The polar bear lives where it is always cold. But he is well-suited to his world. Everything about him is designed to protect him from the cold.

Coloring

The white fur of the polar bear blends in well with the snow. Since there is usually snow in cold places, the polar bear is hard to see. His enemies cannot easily find him.

Fur and Skin

Under his skin the polar bear has a layer of fat to help keep him warm in cold weather. His fur is thick and dense to help keep the cold and water away from his skin.

Now go back and read the entire story.
Then answer the questions below.

1. What is the polar bear's world like? _____

   _____

2. How does the polar bear's coloring protect him?

   _____

3. How is the polar bear's body well-suited to his world ?

   _____

   _____

Study Questions

Sometimes an author puts **study questions** at the beginning or end of a story. Reading the study questions *first* can help you understand the story.

Read the **study questions** below. They are about fleas. If you already know the answers, write them in the spaces provided.

1. How many wings do fleas have?_____

2. Why are fleas dangerous? _____

_____

_____

3. How does a flea get to a new host? _____

_____

_____

4. What is the best way to protect against fleas?_____

_____

_____

Now read the story on the next page.

Fleas

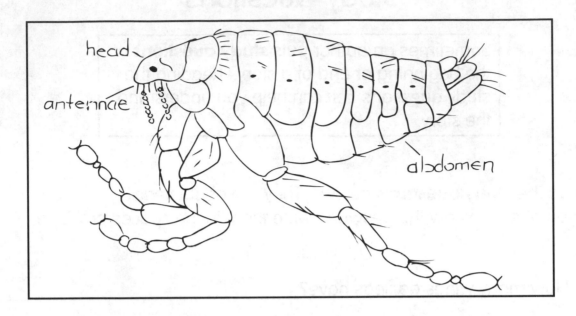

Fleas are one of the most common pests of the civilized world. Fleas need blood for food, so they puncture the skin with their beaks. They are dangerous pests because they can carry diseases from one animal to another.

Fleas do not have wings for flying, but because they have strong legs, they are excellent jumpers. The kind that lives on dogs can jump 13 inches (33 centimeters). This allows the flea to jump from from one host animal to another.

The best protections against fleas are cleanliness and proper care of pets. If you keep your pet's living area dusted with flea powder, you may never need to give your pet a flea bath.

Now go back to the previous page. Answer the questions you didn't answer before you read the story. Correct any incorrect answers you wrote before you read the story.

Answer Key

Please take time to go over the work your child has completed. Ask your child to explain what he/she has done. Praise both success and effort. If mistakes have been made, explain what the answer should have been and how to find it. Let your child know that mistakes are a part of learning. The time you spend with your child helps let him/her know you feel learning is important.

page 1

It is important to know the following in order to understand what you read:
- **Who** is the story about?
- **What** happened in the story?
- **Where** did it happen?
- **When** did it happen?

A Baby Panda

One special day in April, far away in China, a baby panda was born. The tiny panda weighed only about four ounces (113 grams), and her eyes were closed. Even though the baby panda grew quickly, she was helpless for a long time.

When she was three months old, she had hair and could crawl. By the time the baby was seven months old, she was able to run, climb, and begin eating bamboo. In about a year she would be ready to leave her mother.

1. Who is the story about?
   a baby panda
2. Where did the story take place?
   in China
3. When did the story happen?
   in April
4. What was happening to the baby panda?
   She was growing up

page 2

Visitors from Space

It was 2:00 in the morning when Robot M6-D6 landed his spacecraft outside Greg's window. The pale-green light from the spacecraft's anti-gravity blasters caused Greg to wake up. He peered carefully through the window and tried to decide if he should go outside. As he watched, a silver ramp dropped from the bottom of the spacecraft and out rolled M6-D6.

Soon Greg's curiosity was too much for him. He crept out to get a closer look at the visitor. Greg hid behind the woodpile and watched as M6-D6 rolled around the yard picking up samples of rocks and small plants.

As Greg leaned over the woodpile to get a closer look, he knocked over several pieces of wood. The noise startled M6-D6 and he began to beep loudly. The robot hurried to the spacecraft. A moment later, the yard was lit by a pale-green glow. Soon the spacecraft was gone.

1. Who are the characters in this story?
   Greg and the robot M6-D6
2. When did the story take place?
   at 2:00 in the morning
3. What caused Greg to wake up?
   a pale green light
4. Where did the spacecraft land?
   outside Greg's window
5. What was the purpose of M6-D6's trip to Earth?
   to get samples of rocks and plants
6. What caused M6-D6 to leave so suddenly?
   a noise startled him when the wood fell

page 3

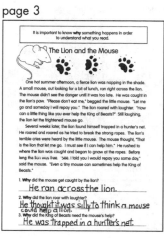

The Lion and the Mouse

One hot summer afternoon, a fierce lion was napping in the shade. A small mouse, out looking for a bit of lunch, ran right across the lion. The mouse didn't see the danger until it was too late. He was caught in the lion's paw. "Please don't eat me," begged the little mouse. "Let me go and someday I will repay you." The lion roared with laughter. "How can a little thing like you ever help the King of Beasts?" Still laughing, the lion let the frightened mouse go.

Several weeks later, the lion found himself trapped in a hunter's net. He roared and roared as he tried to break the strong ropes. The lion's terrible cries were heard by the little mouse. The mouse thought, "That is the lion that let me go. I must see if I can help him." He rushed to where the lion was caught and began to gnaw at the ropes. Before long the lion was free. "See, I told you I would repay you some day," said the mouse. "Even a tiny mouse can sometimes help the King of Beasts."

1. Why did the mouse get caught by the lion?
   He ran across the lion.
2. Why did the lion roar with laughter?
   He thought it was silly to think a mouse could help a lion.
3. Why did the King of Beasts need the mouse's help?
   He was trapped in a hunter's net.

page 5

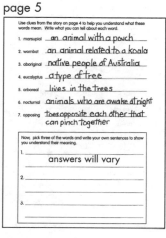

Use clues from the story on page 4 to help you understand what these words mean. Write what you can tell about each word.

1. marsupial **an animal with a pouch**
2. wombat **an animal related to a koala**
3. aboriginal **native people of Australia**
4. eucalyptus **a type of tree**
5. arboreal **lives in the trees**
6. nocturnal **animals who are awake at night**
7. opposing **toes opposite each other that can pinch together**

Now, pick three of the words and write your own sentences to show you understand their meaning.

1. **answers will vary**
2.
3.

page 7

Paragraph 1

Main Idea: The two kinds of African rhinos are different in several ways.

Supporting Details: **One is black. It browses and uses its long upper lip to grab food. One is white. It uses its squared off mouth to graze or grass.**

Paragraph 2

Main Idea: Rhinos are unusual looking animals.

Supporting Details: **It has a wrinkled nose, 2 vertical horns, short clumsy looking legs, thick rough skin, and an immense body.**

Paragraph 3

Main Idea: Rhinos are not slow and clumsy.

Supporting Details: **Rhinos can run as fast as a horse for short distances.**

Paragraph 4

Main Idea: Rhinos are most active at night.

Supporting Details: **It eats grass, leafy twigs and shrubs during the night. It rests during the day.**

page 9

Number these sentences about **The Science Project** in the order they happened in the story.

- **3** After several days the tadpoles began to hatch.
- **5** On Friday, Jose took his science project to school.
- **6** Mr. Nielsen liked Jose's science project.
- **1** Jose found frog eggs in the pond and took some home in a jar.
- **4** The young tadpoles had gills, but no mouth.
- **2** Each day the black part of the eggs grew to look more like a tadpole.

Make a drawing to illustrate Jose's science project.

answers will vary

page 10

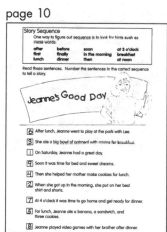

Story Sequence
One way to figure out sequence is to look for hints such as these words:

after	before	soon	at 3 o'clock
first	finally	in the morning	breakfast
lunch	dinner	then	at noon

Read these sentences. Number the sentences in the correct sequence to tell a story.

Jeanne's Good Day

- **6** After lunch, Jeanne went to play at the park with Lee.
- **3** She ate a big bowl of oatmeal with raisins for breakfast.
- **1** On Saturday, Jeanne had a great day.
- **9** Soon it was time for bed and sweet dreams.
- **4** Then she helped her mother make cookies for lunch.
- **2** When she got up in the morning, she put on her best shirt and shorts.
- **7** At 4 o'clock it was time to go home and get ready for dinner.
- **5** For lunch, Jeanne ate a banana, a sandwich, and three cookies.
- **8** Jeanne played video games with her brother after dinner.

page 11

Cause and Effect
A **cause** is what makes something happen.
Not looking where I was going **caused** me to run into the door.
An **effect** is what happened.
The **effect** of not looking was that I ran into the door.

It is important to understand what **effects** are caused by events in the story. To find the **cause**, ask yourself,
"*Why did this happen?*"

Read these sentences.
LOOK for the cause and the effect.

1. After the rain, there were many accidents on the slick streets of the city.
   cause - **rain on the streets**
   effect - **accidents**
2. Polly knew the water was boiling when she heard the teakettle whistle.
   cause - **water was boiling**
   effect - **tea kettle whistled**
3. Toby had to be taken to the hospital after he fell out of the tall tree in his backyard.
   cause - **Toby fell out of a tree.**
   effect - **He had to go to the hospital.**

page 12

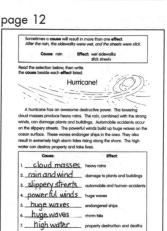

Sometimes a **cause** will result in more than one **effect**.
After the rain, the sidewalks were wet, and the streets were slick.

Cause: rain   **Effect:** wet sidewalks
                            slick streets

Read the selection below, then write the **cause** beside each **effect** listed.

Hurricane!

A hurricane has an awesome destructive power. The towering cloud masses produce heavy rains. The rain, combined with the strong winds, can damage plants and buildings. Automobile accidents occur on the slippery streets. The powerful winds build up huge waves on the ocean surface. These waves endanger ships in the area. They also result in extremely high storm tides rising along the shore. The high water can destroy property and take lives.

Cause:	Effect:
1. **cloud masses**	heavy rains
2. **rain and wind**	damage to plants and buildings
3. **slippery streets**	automobile and human accidents
4. **powerful winds**	huge waves
5. **huge waves**	endangered ships
6. **huge waves**	storm tides
7. **high water**	property destruction and deaths

page 15

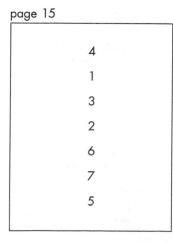

4
1
3
2
6
7
5

page 16

1. Plants were disappearing.
2. They waited in the dark until they heard a crunching sound. They shined a light at the sound and saw a tortoise. Dad put it in a hamster cage.
3. Hercules was probably brought to the area from a desert, then abandoned by its owners.
4. When they are in a cooler climate, tortoises get a virus that will kill other tortoises if they go back to the desert.
5. Hercules went to live with other tortoises at the animal shelter.

page 17

hornet	snail
bee	lamb
pig	ox
fox	mouse
mule	duck
bug	

1.
2. Answers will vary
3.

page 18

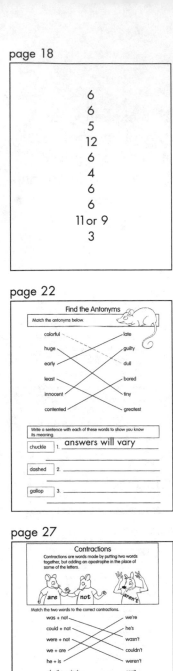

6
6
5
12
6
4
6
6
11 or 9
3

page 19

Symbols
will vary.

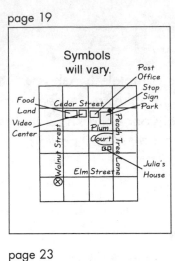

Post Office
Stop Sign
Park
Food Land
Video Center
Cedar Street
Peach Tree Lane
Plum Court
Walnut Street
Julia's House
Elm Street

page 20

Find the Synonym

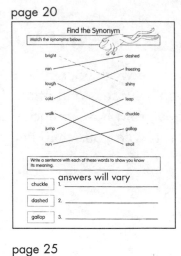

Match the synonyms below.

bright — shiny
ran — dashed
laugh — chuckle
cold — freezing
walk — stroll
jump — leap
run — gallop

Write a sentence with each of these words to show you know its meaning.

chuckle — 1. answers will vary
dashed — 2.
gallop — 3.

page 21

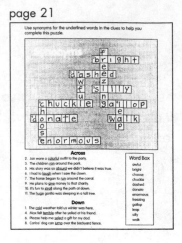

Use synonyms for the underlined words in the clues to help you complete this puzzle.

frezing
bright
dashed
wful
silly
chuckle gallop
donate walk
hos
enormous

Across
2. Jan wore a colorful outfit to the party.
3. The children ran around the park.
5. His story was so absurd we didn't believe it was true.
6. I had to laugh when I saw the clown.
7. The horse began to run around the corral.
8. He plans to give money to their friends.
10. It's fun to stroll along the path at dawn.
11. The huge gorilla was sleeping in a tall tree.

Down
1. The cold weather told us winter was here.
4. Max felt terrible after he yelled at his friend.
6. Please help me select a gift for my dad.
9. Carlos' dog can jump over the backyard fence.

Word Box
awful
bright
choose
chuckle
dashed
donate
enormous
freezing
gallop
leap
silly
walk

page 22

Find the Antonyms

Match the antonyms below.

colorful — dull
huge — tiny
early — late
least — greatest
innocent — guilty
contented — bored

Write a sentence with each of these words to show you know its meaning.

chuckle — 1. answers will vary
dashed — 2.
gallop — 3.

page 23

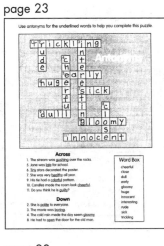

Use antonyms for the underlined words to help you complete this puzzle.

trickling
rude
cheerful
early
huge
sick
dull
gloomy
innocent

Antonyms

Across
1. The stream was rushing over the rocks.
5. Jane was late for school.
6. Tiny stars decorated the poster.
7. She was very healthy all year.
9. His tie had a colorful pattern.
10. Candles made the room look cheerful.
11. Do you think he is guilty?

Down
2. She is polite to everyone.
3. The movie was boring.
4. The cold rain made the day seem gloomy.
6. He had to open the door for the old man.

Word Box
cheerful
close
dull
early
gloomy
huge
innocent
interesting
rude
sick
trickling

page 25

Fill in the blanks. Use the homophones on the previous page to help you fill in the blanks.

1. Did the cut on your heel heal yet?
2. I cannot loan you the lone dollar in my pocket!
3. If you bury the ripe berry no one can eat it.
4. The male lion's mane is his main feature.
5. Please haul those things from the hall to the garage.
6. A special collar will cause the fleas to flee from your dog.
7. Please pour some lotion on my hand to soften the pore of my skin.
8. Take a poll of the class opinions and post it on that pole.

page 26

Compound Words

Compound words are made of two smaller words put together.

wheel + chair = wheelchair
grand + mother = grandmother
holy + day = holiday

Put two words together to make new words.

basket + ball = basketball
cheer + leader = cheerleader
wild + life = wildlife
house + work = housework
high + way = highway
news + cast = newscast
week + end = weekend
wood + land = woodland
home + made = homemade
who + ever = whoever
touch + down = touchdown
under + ground = underground
ware + house = warehouse
well - l + fare = welfare

page 27

Contractions

Contractions are words made by putting two words together, but adding an apostrophe in the place of some of the letters.

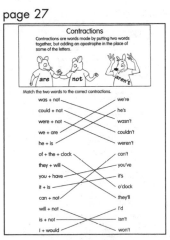

are   not   aren't

Match the two words to the correct contractions.

was + not — wasn't
could + not — couldn't
were + not — weren't
we + are — we're
he + is — he's
of + the + clock — o'clock
they + will — they'll
you + have — you've
it + is — it's
can + not — can't
will + not — won't
is + not — isn't
I + would — I'd

page 28

Prefixes

A **prefix** is added to the beginning of a word.
A **prefix** can change the meaning of a word.

interesting becomes **un**interesting

The prefixes **un**, **in** and **im** mean **not** and, when added to words, change them into their antonym.

Add prefixes to the words below to make **antonyms**, then write the meanings of each new word.

1. in + effective = ineffective
   meaning: not effective

2. im + personal = impersonal
   meaning: not personal

3. un + likely = unlikely
   meaning: not likely

4. un + comfortable = uncomfortable
   meaning: not comfortable

5. in + secure = insecure
   meaning: not secure

6. im + perfect = imperfect
   meaning: not perfect

page 29

Suffix

A suffix is a syllable put at the end of a word to change its meaning or give more information. Here are some common suffixes we use.

ful   less   es   ess   ly   able
est   ology   let   ment   ness   ant

Underline the suffix in these words.

careless   owlet   heaviest   slowly
speechless   watchful   happiness   careful
profitable   bosses   servant   sadness
happily   biology   quickest   governess

Write the words next to the clues.

watchful — keeping an eye on things
speechless — unable to talk
profitable — successful business
owlet — a small owl
happiness — a state of pleasure
quickest — most rapid
sadness — sorrow
heaviest — weighs the most
slowly — not very quick

page 36

Complete Sentences

A **complete sentence** tells:
• who or what the sentence is about
• the **action** that is taking place

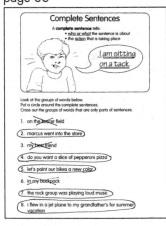

I am sitting on a tack.

Look at the groups of words below.
Put a circle around the complete sentences.
Cross out the groups of words that are only parts of sentences.

1. on the soccer field
2. (marcus went into the store)
3. my best friend
4. (do you want a slice of pepperoni pizza)
5. (let's paint our bikes a new color)
6. in my backpack
7. (the rock group was playing loud music)
8. (i flew in a jet plane to my grandfather's for summer vacation)

page 37

Sentences

There are four kinds of sentences:
Statements tell or state something:
Toni went to the park after school.

Questions ask something:
Did Toni go to the park after school yesterday?

Command sentences command or make a request:
Don't go to the park today. Be careful.

Exclamations show strong emotion:
Going to the park after school is a great idea!

On the line after each sentence, write the kind of sentence it is. Put the correct punctuation at the end of each sentence.

[.] - statement and command
[?] - question
[!] - exclamation

1. Is the cheetah the fastest land animal ? question
2. We enjoyed our trip to the olympics . statement
3. Begin your science projects this week . comand
4. Don't go so close to that steep cliff ! exclamation
5. Have you studied about dinosaurs in school ? question
6. Where do gray whales go in the winter ? question

page 38

Run-on Sentences

A **run-on** sentence is two sentences together without end punctuation to separate them.

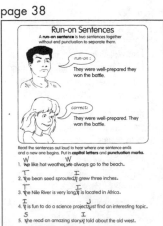

run-on: They were well-prepared they won the battle.

correct: They were well-prepared. They won the battle.

Read the sentences out loud to hear where one sentence ends and a new one begins. Put in **capital letters** and **punctuation marks**.

W   W
We like hot weather we always go to the beach.
T   T
The bean seed sprouted just grew three inches.
T   I
The Nile River is very long it is located in Africa.
I   I
It is fun to do a science project just find an interesting topic.
S   I
She read an amazing story it told about the old west.

page 39

The Strange Planet

Read the story out loud to hear where one sentence ends and a new one begins. Place **punctuation marks** and **capital letters** in this story.

W   I
What a strange place this is. It doesn't look
anything like Earth. Why is the sky so dark and the
ground so bumpy?
W   I
What's that? I saw a furry shape dart behind the
rocks over there. It's moving closer. Help! I can't get away.
M   C
My feet are caught in some weird sticky ooze. Can
anyone hear me?
W   I
Wow! What a scary dream that was. I'm glad to be
awake. That's the last time I have a peanut butter and
pickle sandwich before I go to bed!

page 40

Subject and Predicate

Every sentence has two main parts:
The **subject** tells who or what the sentence is about.
The **predicate** tells what the subject does.

subject
Snow White and the seven dwarves ate dinner together.

predicate
The seven dwarves ate all of the delicious dinner.

Draw one line under the **subject**.
Draw two lines under the **predicate**.

1. The tiny insects scurried quickly from place to place.
2. Matt liked the peace and calm of the forest.
3. The pioneers in their covered wagons faced many dangers.
4. The natives of the tiny village celebrated with a great feast.
5. The dense, tropical rain forests of Brazil are disappearing.
6. The children in the class screamed for the winning team.

Write a sentence of your own. Underline its subject and predicate.

answers will vary

page 41

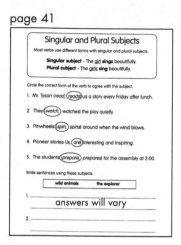

Singular and Plural Subjects

Most verbs use different forms with singular and plural subjects.

Singular subject - The girl sings beautifully.
Plural subject - The girls sing beautifully.

Circle the correct form of the verb to agree with the subject.

1. Mr. Tyson (read, (reads)) us a story every Friday after lunch.
2. They (watch), watches) the play quietly.
3. Pinwheels ((spin), spins) around when the wind blows.
4. Pioneer stories (is, (are)) interesting and inspiring.
5. The students ((prepare), prepares) for the assembly at 2:00.

Write sentences using these subjects.

wild animals	the explorer

1. answers will vary
2.

page 42

Proper Nouns

All nouns name people, places, and things. A proper noun names a particular person, place, or thing and begins with a capital letter.

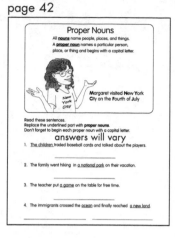

Margaret visited New York City on the Fourth of July

Read these sentences.
Replace the underlined part with proper nouns.
Don't forget to begin each proper noun with a capital letter.

answers will vary

1. The children traded baseball cards and talked about the players.
2. The family went hiking in a national park on their vacation.
3. The teacher put a game on the table for free time.
4. The immigrants crossed the ocean and finally reached a new land.

page 43

Plural Nouns

Most plural nouns end in s, but some nouns form their plurals differently.

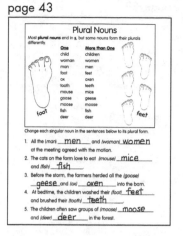

One	More than One
child	children
woman	women
man	men
foot	feet
ox	oxen
tooth	teeth
mouse	mice
goose	geese
moose	moose
fish	fish
deer	deer

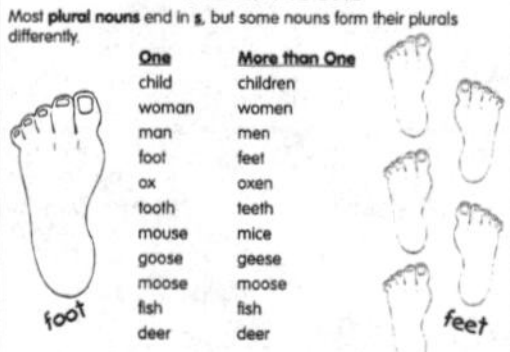

Change each singular noun in the sentences below to its plural form.

1. All the (man) men and (woman) women at the meeting agreed with the motion.
2. The cats on the farm love to eat (mouse) mice and (fish) fish.
3. Before the storm, the farmers herded all the (goose) geese and (ox) oxen into the barn.
4. At bedtime, the children washed their (foot) feet and brushed their (tooth) teeth.
5. The children often saw groups of (moose) moose and (deer) deer in the forest.

page 44

Pronouns

Pronouns take the place of a noun. They are used:

1. in the place of the subject
I you she he it we they
2. to show ownership
my mine your yours his hers our ours their theirs
3. to receive the action of the verb or preposition
me you her him us them

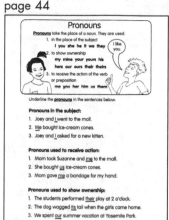

Underline the pronouns in the sentences below.

Pronouns in the subject:
1. Joey and I went to the mall.
2. We bought ice-cream cones.
3. Joey and I asked for a new kitten.

Pronouns used to receive action:
1. Mom took Suzanne and me to the mall.
2. She bought us ice-cream cones.
3. Mom gave me a bandage for my hand.

Pronouns used to show ownership:
1. The students performed their play at 2 o'clock.
2. The dog wagged its tail when the girls came home.
3. We spent our summer vacation at Yosemite Park.

page 45

Adjectives

Adjectives are words that describe a noun or pronoun telling what kind, how many, or which one

green	enormous	Italian
eleven	none	terrified

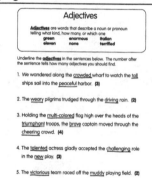

Underline the adjectives in the sentences below. The number after the sentence tells how many adjectives you should find.

1. We wandered along the crowded wharf to watch the tall ships sail into the peaceful harbor. (3)
2. The weary pilgrims trudged through the driving rain. (2)
3. Holding the multi-colored flag high over the heads of the triumphant troops, the brave captain moved through the cheering crowd. (4)
4. The talented actress gladly accepted the challenging role in the new play. (3)
5. The victorious team raced off the muddy playing field. (2)
6. Throughout the long, stormy night, the excited campers shared ghost stories and old legends of mysterious events occuring in the ancient valley. (7)

page 46

Adverbs

An adverb describes the action of the verb, telling how, when, or where the action happened. Many times adverbs end with y or ly.

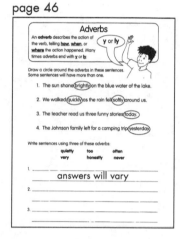

Draw a circle around the adverbs in these sentences. Some sentences will have more than one.

1. The sun shone (brightly) on the blue water of the lake.
2. We walked (quickly) as the rain fell (softly) around us.
3. The teacher read us three funny stories (today).
4. The Johnson family left for a camping trip (yesterday).

Write sentences using three of these adverbs:

quietly	too	often
very	honestly	never

1. answers will vary
2.
3.

page 47

Commas

Use commas to separate:

- items in a series
We ate **apples, dates, and nuts.**
- beginning words such as **yes, no,** and **well**
Well, we might go to Yosemite.
- the person being addressed
Susan, please bring me that tray.

Add commas where they are needed in the following sentences:

1. No, they have not finished their homework yet.
2. We need to buy shirts, pants, socks, and shoes for school.
3. Well, you certainly did a good job on your science project.
4. Remember to bring your raincoat, umbrella, and hat.
5. Sam, were you scared during that horror movie?

Write two sentences of your own that use commas.

1. answers will vary
2.

page 48

"When Someone Speaks"

- Use quotation marks and a comma whenever you are repeating someone's exact words.

Mrs. Torres said, "Please close the door."

- Notice that a comma separates the words being spoken from the rest of the sentence.

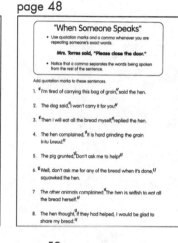

Add quotation marks to these sentences.

1. "I'm tired of carrying this bag of grain," said the hen.
2. The dog said, "I won't carry it for you."
3. "Then I will eat all the bread myself," replied the hen.
4. The hen complained, "It is hard grinding the grain into bread."
5. The pig grunted, "Don't ask me to help!"
6. "Well, don't ask me for any of the bread when it's done!" squawked the hen.
7. The other animals complained, "The hen is selfish to eat all the bread herself."
8. The hen thought, "If they had helped, I would be glad to share my bread."

page 49

Colons and Periods

A colon is used when writing the salutation of a business letter and to separate the hour from minutes when writing the time.

Dear Dr. Smith: **5:25 P.M.**

Add colons where they are needed in this letter.

> Dear Professor Patterson:
>
> Thank you for your help on my project. I will meet you at your office at 6:00.
>
> Sincerely,
> Jason Johnson

Use a period at the end of every abbreviation.

Prof. Salinas **Mr. Edwards**

Add periods after the abbreviations in these sentences.

1. Rev. Madison asked Ms. Swanson to help him lead the singing.
2. Mr. and Mrs. Jamison left their keys in Ms. Smith's car.
3. The students in Mr. Jackson's class submitted their project to Prof. Lowell to be judged.
4. The technician, Ms. Rawlings, fixed our computer on Friday.

page 50

Alphabetical Order

You need to use alphabetical order to locate information in many kinds of reference sources. Pages 1 - 4 help you practice this skill.

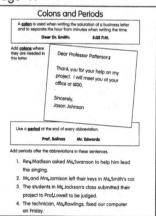

Rewrite these animal names in alphabetical order.

zebra	1.	alligator
badger	2.	badger
walrus	3.	dolphin
ferret	4.	ferret
alligator	5.	gorilla
yak	6.	hippopotamus
pelican	7.	newt
gorilla	8.	pelican
newt	9.	salamander
dolphin	10.	walrus
hippopotamus	11.	yak
salamander	12.	zebra

page 51

Alphabetical Challenge

- When the first and second letters are the same - look at the third letter.
- When the first, second, and third letters are the same - look at the fourth letter.

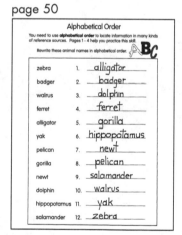

Set 1:	Set 2:
crocus	prepare
crate	preacher
crustacean	prevent
crystal	present
creature	prey
criminal	precious
1. crate	1. preacher
2. creature	2. precious
3. criminal	3. prepare
4. crocus	4. present
5. crustacean	5. prevent
6. crystal	6. prey

page 52

Using a Thesaurus

When you want to use a new word in place of one you already know, look in a thesaurus.

A thesaurus lists synonyms (words with similar meanings).

Use the thesaurus on page 15 to find a new word to replace the underlined words in the sentences below.

1. Thomas felt great fear as he approached the cave.
new word - answers will vary
2. We saw a white figure moving across the lawn at midnight.
new word -
3. The students like their new teacher.
new word -
4. Cheetahs are very fast animals.
new word -
5. Throw the ball to first base.
new word -
6. Take off that wet jacket.
new word -
7. We handled the kittens with care.
new word -

page 54

Parts of a Book

Most nonfiction books have several parts which help you find information.

- **Table of Contents**
This is at the beginning of the book. It lists the titles of the chapters and tells you the page on which each chapter begins.
- **Index**
This is at the end of the book. It lists the topics in the book in alphabetical order and gives you the pages on which you will find each topic mentioned.
- **Glossary**
This is usually found at the back of the book. It gives the meanings for important words you need to understand as you read the book.

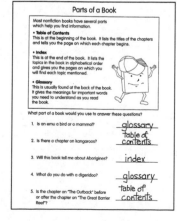

What part of a book would you use to answer these questions?

1. Is an emu a bird or a mammal? glossary
2. Is there a chapter on kangaroos? table of contents
3. Will this book tell me about Aborigines? index
4. What do you do with a digeridoo? glossary
5. Is the chapter on "The Outback" before or after the chapter on "The Great Barrier Reef"? table of contents

page 55

Using a Table of Contents

Table of Contents

Chapter 1: Parts of a River 3
Chapter 2: How Rivers Are Formed 17
Chapter 3: Kinds of Rivers 33
Chapter 4: The Importance of Rivers 56
Chapter 5: Famous Rivers 72

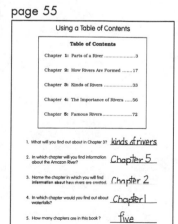

1. What will you find out about in Chapter 3? kinds of rivers
2. In which chapter will you find information about the Amazon River? Chapter 5
3. Name the chapter in which you will find information about how rivers are created. Chapter 2
4. In which chapter would you find out about waterfalls? Chapter 1
5. How many chapters are in this book? five

page 56

Using an Index

Rivers **Index**

Amazon River 76
basin 18
banks 5
canyons 10
cataracts 8
cities 57
Colorado River 83
course 4
dams 57
deltas 16
electricity 70
estuaries 12
irrigation 56
levee 60
Nile River 72
seaports 58
silt 21
streams 17
transportation 60
valley 35
waterfall 34
water power 70

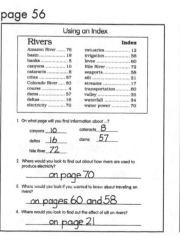

1. On what page will you find information about ...?
canyons 10 cataracts 8
deltas 16 dams 57
Nile River 72
2. Where would you look to find out about how rivers are used to produce electricity?
on page 70
3. Where would you look if you wanted to know about traveling on rivers?
on pages 60 and 58
4. Where would you look to find out the effect of silt on rivers?
on page 21

page 57

Pictures, Captions, and Headings

Authors often give clues about their writing by providing captions for pictures and section headings. Studying these before you begin can help you understand what you are reading.

The polar bear blends well with the white snow around him.

What do you think the story will be about?
answers will vary

Now read only the three headings on the next page.

- What does the first heading tell you about that section?
The section is about the cold places where polar bears live
- What do you think you will learn about in the second section?
I will read about the color of a polar bear
- What does the third heading tell you about the section?
This section tells about a polar bear's fur and skin

The Polar Bear

A Cold World

The polar bear lives where it is always cold. But he is well-suited to his world. Everything about him is designed to protect him from the cold.

Coloring

The white fur of the polar bear blends in well with the snow. Since there is usually snow in cold places, the polar bear is hard to see. His enemies cannot easily find him.

Fur and Skin

Under his skin the polar bear has a layer of fat to help keep him warm in cold weather. His fur is thick and dense to help keep the cold and water away from his skin.

Now go back and read the entire story. Then answer the questions below.

1. What is the polar bear's world like?

It is always cold.

2. How does the polar bear's coloring protect him?

The white fur blends in with the snow.

3. How is the polar bear's body well-suited to his world?

A layer of fat keeps him warm. The thick fur keeps cold and water away.

Study Questions

Sometimes an author puts **study questions** at the beginning or end of a story. Reading the study questions *first* can help you understand the story.

Read the **study questions** below. They are about fleas. If you already know the answers, write them in the spaces provided.

1. How many wings do fleas have? They have no wings.

2. Why are fleas dangerous?

They carry diseases from one animal to another.

3. How does a flea get to a new host?

They jump from the old host to a new host.

4. What is the best way to protect against fleas?

Keep pets and their living area clean. Use flea powder too.

Now read the story on page 15.